BARRY
HUMPHRIES

LESS IS MORE PLEASE

PENGUIN BOOKS

PENGUIN BOOKS

Published by the Penguin Group. Penguin Books Ltd, 27 Wrights Lane, London
w8 5tz, England. Penguin Books USA Inc., 375 Hudson Street, New York,
New York 10014, USA. Penguin Books Australia Ltd, Ringwood, Victoria, Australia.
Penguin Books Canada Ltd, 10 Alcorn Avenue, Toronto, Ontario, Canada m4v 3b2.
Penguin Books (NZ) Ltd, 182 – 190 Wairau Road, Auckland 10, New Zealand · Penguin
Books Ltd, Registered Offices: Harmondsworth, Middlesex, England · This
extract is from *More Please*, by Barry Humphries, first published by Viking 1992.
Published in Penguin Books 1993. This edition published 1996 · Copyright © Barry
Humphries, 1992. All rights reserved · The moral right of the author has been
asserted · Typeset by Rowland Phototypesetting Ltd, Bury St Edmunds, Suffolk.
Printed in England by Clays Ltd, St Ives plc · Except in the United States of America,
this book is sold subject to the condition that it shall not, by way of trade or otherwise,
be lent, re-sold, hired out, or otherwise circulated without the publisher's prior
consent in any form of binding or cover other than that in which it is published and
without a similar condition including this condition being imposed on the subsequent
purchaser · 10 9 8 7 6 5 4 3 2 1

Author's Note: The people portrayed in this book are real and the events described
took place, but fictional names and descriptive detail have sometimes been used.

CONTENTS

Licking the Beaters

Mrs Flint was my very first teacher. I have thought of changing her name in case some litigious descendant recognizes his venerated great-grandmother, but I can find no better name for her than her real name; grey quartzy sharp-edged hard. She ran a small kindergarten in her own grey pebble-dashed Californian bungalow down the hill from our place, and her two best rooms, the lounge and dining-room to the right of her dark hallway, had been turned into a classroom for local tots. Edna, my first and favourite nanny, would escort me every morning down the steep pavement of Marlborough Avenue until after several twists and turns and carefully crossed, sparsely motored roads we arrived at Mrs Flint's front gate, already jammed with tricycles and mothers. Mrs Flint, wearing a large apron to keep the chalk off her faded if floral print dress, stood on the front step screwing her face into what she imagined to be a friendly and motherly grimace as she welcomed her little pupils and reassured departing parents. She was a good actress, this old battle-axe, for the mothers all went home fondly believing that their littlies were in wonderful hands in spite of the panic-stricken screams that most of Mrs Flint's pupils emitted as soon as they realized that they had been abandoned to her care. No sooner had the last mother gone and the drone of the last parental sedan faded up Orrong Crescent than Mrs Flint's true mineral nature asserted itself. Once she was alone with her infant charges the ingratiating smile of the kindly old widow who adored children quickly faded and she would swing around from her blackboard and exhibit to the class a very different and frightening countenance on which rage, spite and ignorance jostled for supremacy.

It always took a long time for the crying to stop at Mrs Flint's kindergarten. One little girl called Jocelyn cried all the time and no amount of cajolery could stop her. In the end Mrs Flint put her out to graze in the back yard where, still bawling, she executed endless circuits on her trike. Inside we sat at miniature tables on stools enamelled cherry-red, one of the most popular hues of the late thirties. Because the classroom occupied Mrs Flint's lounge and dining room there were a few of her more substantial pieces of furniture – a Genoa-velvet couch, a bookcase and a Jacobean-style dining table with matching sideboard – shoved against the wall to make room for our small chairs and tables. Mrs Flint made it very clear that if anyone so much as laid a curious finger on one of her trumpery treacle-coloured sticks they would be put out in the yard with the eternally blubbering Jocelyn.

Mrs Flint was no great reader; except for the *Pears Cyclopaedia*, a couple of Ethel M. Dells and a Netta Muskett, her bookshelves accommodated faded family snaps and gewgaws which she called her 'ordiments'. However, every morning, seated in one of her deeper fawn-and-russet Genoa-velvet lounge chairs, with her dress hitched up so we could see her surgical stockings, she read us a story. Her favourite was Hansel and Gretel and even the least imaginative child found a painful empathy with this tale and its themes of parental abandonment and persecution by a cannibalistic crone.

There was a mid-morning break and we all filed out the back to our trikes and lugubriously circled Mrs Flint's prickly lawn. When I first saw Doré's engraving of convicts dismally revolving in their bleak exercise yard, I had only to imagine them with gaily painted Cyclops tricycles and scooters between their shanks to be grimly reminded of playtime at Mrs Flint's.

One day two bikes rammed into each other just in front of me, and my friend Graham Coles fell off his seat and crashed to the ground, breaking his arm. There was a big fuss and Mrs Flint's face nearly ruptured itself, feigning expressions of compassion and concern. Poor Graham's arm wasn't set properly and it had to be operated on again. This operation was not successful however and Graham's arm never grew. Years later when we were no longer the friends we had been in childhood I would see him as he passed our house on his way to Scotch College, one sleeve especially shortened to accommodate his bonsai appendage.

Apart from her fawning attentions to our parents and nannies there was one other human being to whom Mrs Flint displayed an amiable demeanour. Her daughter Nursie. Over half a century later I can only assume that Nursie was a nurse and that she had a real name like everyone else. But Mrs Flint always called her Nursie and something resembling warmth crept into her cold dry voice when she announced Nursie's presence in the house. For Nursie came and went, and we glimpsed her but occasionally sitting at the linoleum-covered kitchen table having a cup of tea, as we filed out to the back verandah for

3

our play lunch. She had plucked eyebrows and a blonde perm which stuck out in a wedge at the back like Garbo's in the last scene in *Queen Christina*, or like the 'art deco' windswept hair-do of the woman whose white glass profile appeared on top of Atlantic petrol pumps; a crude commercial descendant of Lalique's opaline car mascots.

Between sips of Robur tea and puffs on her Du Maurier, Nursie flashed us a flirtatious smile while Mrs Flint fussed about refilling her cup and fetching her ginger nuts and Marie biscuits as though she were a nice person pleased to see her daughter.

Mrs Flint was keen to show parents that their children didn't just listen to stories or ride their bikes in endless circles in her back yard, so she decided we must all learn to count. I must have been the slowest to acquire this doubtful skill, for I remember being kept back while the other children played. Alone amongst the chipped cherry-red stools while Mrs Flint, terribly close so that I could smell her damp surgical stockings and her odour of stale talcum, forced me to count and count and recount until, weeping, I finally stumbled to one hundred. When would Edna come to rescue me? I wondered, peering up towards the lozenged leadlight windows through which grown-ups could be seen on their way to the front porch. But on that dreadful day each shrill chirrup of the doorbell announced someone else's mother, so that I was alone with my tormentor and all those numbers for what seemed like an eternity before deliverance finally came. Since those early struggles with innumeracy – as I believe it is now called – I have shunned every form of mathematics, leaving the counting to accountants and trusted managers, a task they have often performed with a surprising display of imagination.

I am not certain at this distance in time whether, having counted to a century, I graduated from Mrs Flint's Dame School, or whether my mother, detecting my misery, rescued me. I may well have complained, for I remember my mother saying, in her defence, what a 'refined' woman she thought Mrs Flint to be. Already at four years of age I had begun to apprehend that refinement was very often an extenuating virtue; one that excused and eclipsed almost every other unappetizing trait. But it was hard for me to share this adult view of Mrs Flint's refinement. No doubt the hag had once patronized my mother with a long word or an unfamiliar locution – a verbal crooking of the pinky – and had thereafter acquired her dubious epithet.

I preferred to be at home anyway; pampered by Edna and spoilt by Pat Bagott, our gardener and handyman. Pat was my father's favourite employee, and in Australian society of this period he was that great rarity, a childless Roman Catholic. This may have been the main reason why my mother spoke more generously of him and his little wife than she customarily did of their more fecund co-religionists.

As Mrs Flint's saving grace had been refinement, the Bagotts' was their cleanliness, not an attribute my mother's family associated with the adherents of Rome. She had made a point of seeing where the Bagotts lived; in a flat working-class suburb far from our undulant and lawned oasis. And she had pronounced the dwelling 'spotless', '*small, but spotless*'. One of her favourite sayings was: 'You don't have to be well-off to be *particular*,' and she frequently attributed this apophthegm to her late mother, lending it a kind of genealogical veracity. Much as Field-Marshal Goering sought to confer Aryan status on the Jewish tenor Richard Tauber, so my mother spared Pat Bagott her usual strictures against Catholicism. Without knowing it, the spotless and particular Bagotts were granted a unique amnesty; in my mother's eyes at least they were honorary Protestants.

My father was a builder of sturdy suburban villas whose business reached its first peak of success in the years before the Second World War. He built houses in all the popular styles: mock Tudor, Spanish mission, neo-Georgian, Californian bungalow and moderne. In the very late thirties, if the client was especially rich and daring and my father able to procure enough glass building blocks and aubergine-coloured 'manganese' bricks, he would build them a 'jazz moderne' house with curved corner windows, a flat roof, a nautical-looking sun deck and *no front fence!* It is still odd to see in the suburban streets of Melbourne these once startling architectural hybrids; chubby colonial relations of their austere German cousins in Dessau and Stuttgart.

As a toddler, long before Mrs Flint's kindergarten, I would often be taken off by my father on his daily rounds visiting building sites. In that epoch before seat-belts I would roll around on the back seat of his streamlined putty-white Oldsmobile, or stand precariously on the hot grey leather clinging to a sturdy tassel. We would arrive at a 'job' and while my father strode fearlessly across the raw yellow joists remonstrating with brickies, or pored over flapping blueprints with the foreman, I would amuse myself with a drill and an offcut of Oregon pine. Sometimes we would arrive during the lunch break and I would see the men rolling their 'smokes' and making their billy tea over a mound of blazing wood chips on an improvised hearth. Just as the water in the blackened tin came to the boil Alec Gibson would open a sachet of wax paper his wife had packed with his doorstep sandwiches, and fling the contents of sugar and tea-leaves into the seething water.

I used to love watching the cement being mixed, as I enjoyed a similar process at home when my mother ran up a sponge. Fascinated, I watched the brickies laying a parapet, and, with deft trowels, slicing off the frills of the wet mortar. Alec warned me against getting too near the concrete mixer with a story about a nipper who had only the other day got too close to the grey-lipped maw of that relentlessly sloshing drum, and got sucked in. With a calloused finger he pointed to a small cement-encrusted boot lying amongst the builders' debris. 'That's all that's left of him, Bun,' said Alec lugubriously, 'so don't get too near that bloody doover, or *you'll* be a goner yesself!'

Alec and Pat Bagott and the other men called me 'Bun', which was probably short for currant bun; a reference to my innumerable moles. One day, at smoko, while we were sitting around on piles of bricks, eating our sandwiches and waiting for the billy to boil, Alec stood up, 'See you in a jiff, Bun, just going to strain the potatoes.' And he ambled off in the direction of the narrow galvanized iron dunny, screened with a hessian curtain. That night at dinner I rather pointedly left the table and on the way to the lavatory I called back to my mother, 7

'Just off to strain the potatoes.' When I returned there was an 'atmosphere' and I overheard my mother saying in the low voice children are not supposed to hear, '. . . and just make sure the more common element amongst your men watch what they say in front of little Barry, or who knows what he'll be coming out with next'.

The South Camberwell State School was a raw red-brick two-storey building in a small street off Toorak Road. It stood in an extensive asphalt wasteland, bounded by the palings of adjacent houses. This was the playground. Far away, against the back fence and partly shaded by a mutilated peppercorn, stood the only other structure in that desolate schoolground, the shelter shed. This was a sort of wooden box with one wall missing in which children presumably sheltered from the extremes of the Melbourne climate. At lunchtime on a wet day it would be packed with damp urchins delving into their sandwich tins and screaming at the tops of their voices. The noise in that confined space under a reboant tin roof was appalling, but worse was the overpowering and nauseating stench of gooey brown banana sandwiches and other nameless fillings. It did not surprise me in the least, when years later I learnt that the artless expression, 'Who opened their lunch?' was 1930s Australian slang for 'Who farted?' Only then did I realize that others before me had reeled back from the effluvia of cut lunches.

My parents sent me there for about a year until I was old enough to attend a nice Junior School. I had seen the brochure for Camberwell Grammar in my father's den. It had a sky-blue crinkly cover, embossed with the school's mitred crest, and glossy pages with pictures of some brand-new manganese brick buildings photographed from oblique angles to make them look more monumental than they actually were. It was supposed to be a 'very good school' and it charged *fees*. It catered for boys only, and mostly boys from 'comfortable homes'.

But Camberwell State, which I was forced to attend in the meantime, was free and co-ed. The hardships of life in Mrs Flint's back-yard jungle were nothing compared with the shrieking, thumping, yelling, wrestling maelstrom of human maggots into which I had been hurled.

Quickly I became aware of the gulf that divided me from them; the gulf that separated the Australian working class from the newly arisen 'affluent' middle class. It was wider, bleaker and more inimical than the grey tundra of the playground. In my effeminate little blue Aertex shirt which laced at the neck, pleated linen shorts, fawn cotton socks and leather sandals with side buckles, I felt uncomfortably alien to the other boys. Many of them wore scuffed and splitting sandshoes and a few even arrived at school barefoot. Our classroom was full of densely darned and threadbare maroon sweaters, patched britches, grubby lacunose stockings, scabby knees, bloody noses, verminous hair and ears erupting with bright pumpkin wax. The slatternly girls were no less alarming to a mollycoddled little Lord Fauntleroy from the Golf Links Estate.

The first form was presided over by a gorgon called Miss Jensen. She was the first woman I ever met with her hair in a bun, and she had a knack of making the chalk squeal on the blackboard. She favoured bottle-green 'twin sets' and fawn tweed skirts and she looked uncannily like Mrs Bun the Baker's wife in Happy Families. Miss Jensen and I took an instant dislike to one another.

We lived only about half a mile from the school, so I was mostly spared the ordeal of sandwiches in the shelter shed. Instead, punctually at 12.30, my father would collect me in the big putty-white Oldsmobile and drive me home for a peaceful lunch at my own little table on the lawn, or with my mother in the sun-room amongst her new cane furniture and shining brass knick-knacks. Everything in our house was new, or 'up-to-date' as they said in the thirties. We had a new Frigidaire with a light inside which went on when you opened the door. Every now and then it shuddered rather violently, as if from the cold. Most other people we knew still had ice-chests, and I rather envied them the iceman's visit as he shouldered those great glassy blocks up their sideways. On top of the fridge stood our new Sunbeam Mixmaster. This was a streamlined bullet-shaped appliance rather like a Buck Rogers spaceship, in the popular colour combination of cream and black. We had all the attachments and the brochure, but we only used it for juicing oranges and making cakes. When the twin whisks plunged into the bowl of glutinous sponge mixture my mother tweaked a mammiform control knob to the appropriate speed and the engine whirred into action, the whisks churning so that their blades seemed to vanish until they were just two chrome rods suspended in a fragrant yellow vortex. The kitchen filled with a miraculous aroma of heating machinery, compounded with vanilla essence. Once the Mixmaster was silenced and the whisks detached, I was allowed to lick off the ambrosial emulsion. Licking the beaters was one of the great privileges of an Australian childhood.

Our other modern appliance was a Radiola 'mantel model' wireless set. Chubbily ziggurattish in moulded brown Bakelite, it had a vertically fluted front panel rather like the fascia of a modernistic building. Behind the organ-pipe grille could be glimpsed a curtain of sheeny brown cretonne through which the music and the voices shrilly filtered. 'The Girl on the Pink Police Gazette' and 'My Merry Oldsmobile' were popular airs of the period, and it seemed strange and inexplicable that the radio could be singing so intimately about our family car.

> Come away with me Lucile
> In my merry Oldsmobile,
> Down the road of life we'll fly
> Automobubbling you and I.
> To the church we'll swiftly steal,
> Then our wedding bells will peal,
> You can go as far as you like with me,
> In my merry Oldsmobile.

I had been given a toy submarine made in Japan, containing a clockwork mechanism which, when wound up, propelled it realistically along the bottom of the bath. One day I took it to school, a big mistake. It was one of those rare days when I didn't go home for lunch, so, avoiding the hellish shelter shed, I took my sub and my sandwiches to a peaceful corner of the playground. Soon I found myself encircled by a group of rough kids who demanded my submarine. A tussle ensued in which my lunch got trodden into the asphalt and as the jeering circle 11 of larrikins drew closer and more threatening I picked up a handful of gravel ready to defend myself. The bullies fled, but they did not disperse. They must have formed a delegation to Miss Jensen because immediately after recess she hauled me out in front of the class for 'throwing stones', a heinous violation of the school rules. I denied doing any such thing, but the testimony of the smirking yahoos carried more weight than my tearful protestations, and I was pushed in the corner for the rest of the afternoon with a sign on my back: I AM A BULLY. Much later, when the class had been dismissed for the afternoon, Miss Jensen told me that if I persisted in denying my guilt she would take me to see Mr Fraser, the headmaster, a ginger-haired functionary whom I had privately nicknamed 'Duckface'. I stuck to my guns, however, and only at the entrance to his study, and threatened with imminent expulsion, did I finally break down and recant, confessing to a crime I had never committed. Grudgingly, clemency supervened, and I was allowed to go home, my heart pounding with shame and rage. For some reason which remains obscure, I never told my parents of this incident – perhaps I feared that they might share Miss Jensen's view of the matter.

Since then I have entertained fantasies of vengeance. Supposing Miss Jensen had been, say, twenty-five at the time, she might now, in 1992, be a sprightly seventy-seven-year-old living with her daughter, sitting peacefully knitting in some honeysuckled garden bower, or quietly watching television in a Melbourne suburb. For my purposes it would be more convenient if she were installed in a sunset facility or oldsters' terminary. There I could visit her, explaining to the nursing staff that I was a concerned relation who required a few moments' privacy with the titubating inmate. I would need very little time to attach the small placard, concealed under my raincoat, to the back of old Miss Jensen's bobbing matinée jacket.

Wilf

Uncle Wilf was my favourite uncle. He was married to Aunty
Violet, my mother's oldest sister, who had once been a nurse
and had tended victims of the Spanish influenza just after the
First World War. Wilf had served in the Australian infantry
in France and their house contained a number of souvenirs of
those terrible battles. On their Arts and Crafts mantelpiece
stood two gleaming brass shell-cases and, high up in a cup-
board, Uncle Wilf kept a German helmet with a spike on it.
Sometimes he showed us a sepia photograph taken from the
pocket of a dead German soldier, perhaps the same soldier who
no longer required the helmet. The picture showed a husband
and wife, she seated with a certain wistful beauty, he in uniform
standing stiffly at her side. In the background was the blurred
hint of a bourgeois parlour – no doubt a tricked-up corner of
the photographer's studio. They both gazed apprehensively at
the lens as though it were about to go off like a rifle, but that
would come a month or two later.

Uncle Wilf was the only person I knew who had served
in the First World War, though casualties of that legendary
catastrophe were often pointed out to me; legless lift drivers,
blind newspaper sellers, and the door-to-door salesman from
whom my mother bought our honey who always wore one stiff
black glove.

14 Wilf always marched on 25 April, that most important day

in the Australian calendar, Anzac Day, when a great cavalcade of Diggers walked in solemn procession to the Shrine of Remembrance. Every year we, and thousands of others, would line the roadside and cheer the old soldiers, many in uniform and others in their Sunday best blazing with medals, as the military bands played 'Tipperary', 'Pack Up Your Troubles' and 'Roses of Picardy'. At the end of that long procession came the wheelchairs and the stretchers and nurses leading the gassed and the blind.

Wilf and Vi had one son, who was a spastic, and my aunt and uncle were devoted to his welfare. John loved music and had a large collection of records which he would play loudly at family tea parties. No one listened to his carefully planned recitals, they only talked louder, though occasionally someone would glance over at him as he sat by the gramophone nodding his head to the music, his poor legs in chromium callipers.

'There's no doubt about John,' they would cluck. *'He loves his music.'*

Uncle Wilf worked for Imperial Chemical Industries and my father often took me to his office in the city where I would be given small sample jars of dye manufactured by the company. At home I experimented with these wonderful pigments: purple, fuchsia and gamboge, dropping a pinch or two into a full beaker, and watching the bright streamers of colour fall through the water and spread like tendrils, or making exotically hued potions in the new laboratory which my father had built for me at the back of the garage.

Wilf and my father adored each other, and the three of us would regularly lunch at the Wool Exchange Hotel near Uncle

Wilf's office. It was my first experience of a restaurant, and there was a pretty receptionist who always greeted the brothers-in-law flirtatiously and made a fuss over me as she led us between the rowdy lunchers to our special table. There were stiff, starched napkins, a cruet holding the indispensable bottle of Holbrook's Worcestershire sauce and, in the centre of the table, an oxidized nickel trumpet from which a few crumpled poppies bloomed on their hairy stems. The vegetable fritter with hot tomato sauce was one of the Wool Exchange's gastronomic specialities, as well as the more conservative T-bone steak and crumbed whiting.

It must have been during one of these lunches that the two men planned to build a weekend shack together at Healesville, a beauty spot about forty miles from town. Accordingly they bought thirty acres of virgin bush about a mile from the township, up a dusty track. There, in a small clearing with a blue view of Mount Riddell and the lavender-coloured foothills of the Great Divide, my father, assisted by Pat and Alec, built a house, known thereafter as 'the shack'. It was a rudimentary structure of weatherboard, asbestos sheeting and corrugated iron and there were none of the cosy amenities of Camberwell. No water, electricity or sewerage, so we had a galvanized-iron tank at the side of the house, spirit lamps and an outdoor dunny, built of split logs over a very deep hole. This was furnished with little more than a huge desiccated tarantula on the ceiling and, for the hygienic convenience of visitors, a mutilated Melbourne telephone book suspended by a string from a bent nail. This popular cubicle buzzed perpetually with the sound of voracious flies and reeked of some ammoniac pink powder which Papa Brown regularly ladled into the abyss.

Soon our shack in the bush became a regular weekend haven for all the relations. There were beds everywhere, and at night on my lumpy mattress in my little 'sleep-out', I could hear the adults in the living-room playing Whist and Mah-jong late into the night, smell Uncle Wilf's sweet Wayside Mixture and hear my father pumping up the kerosene lamps until the guttering mantles glowed white again. In the forties we acquired a battery-powered wireless set, and on Sunday evenings everyone listened to the Lux Radio Theatre. There was great excitement if the hour-long melodrama happened to star Thelma Scott, my mother's sole theatrical acquaintance, or Thelma's talented young friend, Coral Browne.

When war came I would lie awake in bed watching the lamplight ebb and flow through the crack under my door and hear those urgent, ominous news reports of far-away catastrophes. The voice of Winston Churchill crackled over the BBC World Service as my family sat gravely listening to the war in the silent Australian bush 13,000 miles from Westminster. There was so much distortion and explosive static on those shortwave broadcasts that I pictured Churchill himself standing at the very heart of the battlefield, perpetually under fire and growling his famous rhetoric through a lethal fusillade.

One night in about 1943 I heard them playing 'Sweet Spirit', a psychic parlour game in which I was never allowed to participate. An alphabetical circle was arranged on the table top and everyone put their finger on an upturned glass in the middle. They all took it in turns to ask the spirit questions, and there were always crescendos of laughter followed by, 'Shhh, you'll wake the children.' My father was regularly reproached for cheating. One night I heard a voice, I think it was Aunty Dorothy's, ask the spirit when Cliff Jones, Phyllis's brother, was coming home on leave, and there was a strange silence in the room as the glass, carrying everyone's fingers with it, darted from N to E to V to E to R. They never played that game again.

In the long summer vacation my father built a log fort for me and a red bark tree-house high up in a shaggy old eucalypt. My tree-house even had an old-fashioned battery-operated telephone connected to the main house, so that I could order cakes and sandwiches without ever having to leave my eyrie. Here I played for hours in my new Gene Autry cowboy suit with its fringed white kid chaps and my Gene Autry ivory-handled cap gun. Watching out for snakes, my young sister and I would explore the bush together, while back at the house cousin John played his portable gramophone, so that wherever we were we could hear from afar those wisps of tinny music like the horns of elfland faintly blowing. It was strange sitting on a mossy log in the Australian bush and listening to Fraser Simpson's incomparable Vocal Gems from *Toad of Toad Hall* or Richard Tauber's 'Dein ist mein ganzes Herz'. Especially strange, really, to hear the illicit language of the Enemy thrillingly wafted through the saplings and the sword grass and the yellow flowering acacias and the mauve bush orchids.

The hour drive to Healesville seemed, of course, interminable to a child. Camberwell was then on the outskirts of the metropolitan area and once past Box Hill we were in open country. Near Lilydale, my father always pointed out the long and impeccably shaved hedge of green privet that concealed from the road the vast estate of Dame Nellie Melba, and Coombe Cottage, the Australian diva's legendary home. Melba and Donald Bradman were the only famous Australians I had ever heard of, and it seemed an amazing coincidence that Melba's name should so closely resemble the city of her birth.

Half-way to the shack we crossed a billabong of the Yarra River on a low pontoon bridge, and there on a kind of island almost camouflaged amongst the tangled blackberries and the sloughed bark of the huge river gums was a small swagman's encampment; a few wretched humpies built from rusty kerosene tins and hessian bags. As our Oldsmobile rolled past, a starved yellow mongrel always started up and barked until we were out of sight. My father had only once pointed to this little camp, but thereafter our noses were pressed to the car windows whenever we approached the river bank in the hope that we might glimpse one of these legendary vagabonds boiling his billy, or stuffing a jumbuck in his tucker bag like the hero of that incomprehensible song 'Waltzing Matilda'.

Half a mile from the shack on the other side of the Don Road lived a real swagman called Smithy. Smithy dwelt in an improvised hovel of galvanized iron and sacking where chooks and dogs scrabbled in the dust. He had a wife somewhere in that kennel too, who was supposed to be, according to Uncle Wilf, 'as black as your hat'. Smithy was a lanky taciturn figure with a pointed Adam's apple, a grey 'Kitchener' moustache and an old digger's hat. He still wore the threadbare remnant of a khaki uniform and after Uncle Wilf befriended him he used to chop wood for us, and do odd jobs. Sometimes I would 19 sit with the men at smoko and hear Smithy tell some of his old soldier's yarns. He had a great and touching nobility, like a peasant in a story by Turgenev. In September, before the morning mist cleared and the magpies were gargling in the tall saplings, Smithy would show us the paddocks where we could find the best and biggest mushrooms. They were the ones with the blue-pink gills underneath: the colour of milky cocoa.

If we were at Healesville at Christmas time, and the heat became unbearable, we would set off with rugs and picnic baskets to Badgers Creek. There, where no badger had ever set foot, amongst the pungent mosses, and sheltered by tall tree ferns, we splashed about in a dark green pool. Then we would perch on the bank watching the icy water purl and gurgle over rocks like emus' eggs, and sip raspberry vinegar from Bakelite cups, while Peter Dawson sang 'The Floral Dance' on John's wind-up phonograph.

There was a terrible week in 1939 when the great bushfires which raged throughout Victoria nearly got the shack. Wilf and my father drove back and forth from Healesville all day, through the smoke and under a dark copper sky, bringing linen and portable furniture to safety. The house and its surroundings, however, were spared, though it was a close one, and on the crest of Mount Riddell there was always, thereafter, a bald white patch of bleached burnt-out timber.

Those bush holidays provide the happiest memories of my childhood, and during the war the house was extended to furnish more bedrooms in case we decided to evacuate there when the bombs fell. For some reason it was felt that thirty-five miles from the General Post Office was a safe radius if the Japanese invaded Melbourne.

In the late 1930s the voice of Joseph Schmidt was always on the wireless, singing that evocative song of the period, 'A Star Fell from Heaven'. It was the voice of Europe before the Terror and, had I but known it, a Jewish voice. But the song which I most associate with the outbreak of war was 'South of the Border (Down Mexico Way)' crooned in the light tenor of Gene Autry. Whenever I am in Los Angeles, supping with my friend Roddy McDowall in Studio City, I gaze across his fence at the house next door where Gene Autry still lives, in the hope that I may catch a glimpse of my childhood idol.

Papa Brown, my maternal grandfather, had an ominous ditty in his music-hall repertoire.

> Tramp, tramp, the boys are marching
> Knock, knock, the bobby's at the door.
> If you don't let him in
> He will knock the door right in,
> And you won't see your daddy any more!

This cautionary refrain gave me terrible nightmares and Papa was forbidden by my mother to sing it ever again. Early in the war I must have overheard many discussions between my parents about whether or not my father should enlist. His younger brother, Dick, had joined the air force and my mother's brother was in the Australian Imperial Force, and I am sure my father, although he was just too old to be called up, had pangs of conscience about not doing 'his bit'. I can remember an argument between my parents once, when we   21 drove past the Hawthorn recruiting station, but Wilf ultimately arranged for my father to do war work for ICI, building munition factories and nitroglycerine storage tanks at Deer Park, an outer Melbourne suburb. However, I am convinced the spectre of conscription must have hung over him during the early war years and I always feared that his father-in-law's minatory recruiting jingle would come true, and that my father might be snatched away by the army and I would never see him again.

When the war broke out he employed several very jolly Italians called the Angelo Brothers who created the terrazzo porches and bathroom floors in all his houses. They seemed to sing all the time as they worked and they wore paper hats made from Geelong Cement bags to keep off the sun. But one day they disappeared and were never spoken of again. Although they had probably lived in Australia for years and had barely heard of Mussolini they were interned for the duration of the war in some dismal concentration camp outside the city. There was also a German carpenter called Fritz whom my father liked, and an attempt was made to save him from the same fate as the Dagos. One day my father asked Fritz to come into his den, put his hand on the family Bible and swear allegiance to King George. Agog, I witnessed this touching if somewhat naïve ceremony but, alas, it failed to save poor old Fritz from his inevitable sequestration.

Unlike my mother, my father sometimes spoke to foreigners, and often told a story of one of his uncles back in Benalla who had befriended a German tradesman during the Great War when the rest of the town refused to talk to him. When he finally died he left Great-Uncle Frank a house and several thousand pounds.

I had embarked on philately and I already had a large collection of British stamps, including a Penny Black. When my grandparents went back to England for the coronation of King George VI, I steamed the stamps off their many letters and postcards. I also had an exciting German section in my album thanks to a funny old lady called Mrs Vennermark who lived a few doors down Marlborough Avenue in a tapestry-brick, neo-Tudor bungalow built for her by my father in 1938. Old Mrs Vennermark – though she was probably only about forty-five – spoke with a strange accent, which gave her an air of acerbity. Her house had quite a few 'teething problems' too, and I often heard her harsh voice on the telephone asking for my father. 'It's that Jewish woman making trouble again,' my mother would say. 'Why your father does business with them I'll never understand.' Mr Friedmann was another thorn in her side. He ran a local firm called the Suburban Timber Supply and although my father liked him, my mother was convinced that he was a cheat and a swindler. However, in spite of my mother's open hostility towards her, old Mrs Vennermark was very kind to me, giving me the stamps off all the letters she received from her family who were still in Germany. They were rather spectacular: most had swastikas on them and images of a bad-tempered-looking man with folded arms and a square moustache. I secretly hoped Mrs Vennermark's family would not come to Melbourne too soon or an important philatelic source might dry up. But as it happened she remained alone, and some time around 1940 the letters stopped.

My parents enjoyed a busy social life. Once a week they had a card night. Baize-topped bridge tables were erected in the 'best' room and my mother spent the whole day making sandwiches and cakes. Her specialities were matches – a delicious colonial millefeuille filled with jam and cream and covered with walnuts – and sponge fingers with passionfruit icing. The next morning we had what was left of the sandwiches toasted for breakfast and took the cakes to school in greaseproof paper.

When my mother took me into town on her shopping expeditions, we usually visited Mitzi of Vienna, her favourite dress shop. The proprietrix, whose creations my mother found irresistible, was another of those exotic arrivals of the late thirties whose companions had given Melbourne chocolates, coffee lounges and chamber music. We would also visit the Myer Emporium, where my mother had once worked as a modiste, before she married my father. I noticed her voice changed when she spoke to the shop assistants, as though she had to make it very clear that she and they were now separated by a great distance, and the gap was getting wider. I always felt uncomfortable when she spoke in that unreal drawl, but I was coming to believe that my mother was perhaps several women; or different things to different people, and there was a life within her which excluded me.

Sometimes we lunched at Myer's in the Mural Hall, which for suburban shoppers of this, or any, period was the height of grandeur. Frequently used for fashion parades and receptions, it was decorated with large pale neo-classical frescoes by Napier Waller, a Melbourne artist who had lost his right arm in the First World War and immediately began painting with his left. More often, however, we had our lunch at the Wattle Tea Rooms in Little Collins Street. The Wattle was a long room in the Arts and Crafts style, with leadlight windows on the street, and dark wainscot within. Plates, Toby jugs and knick-knacks stood on the sempiternal curio ledge, and there were chintzy banquettes to the left and right, and white linen tables down the middle. These dark varnished surroundings emphasized the bright floral dresses and hats of the women who, talced and toilet-watered, thronged the Wattle every day, so that the whole café resembled a conservatory. Women like stocks, in mauve and heliotrope, or puffed up in brighter speckled hues like calceolarias. Blue delphinium women nodded to each other across the room and there were old ladies too, like bunches of violets and boronia huddled behind their Denby Ware tea sets, or sitting alone pecking at asparagus rolls. There was, of course, no shortage of snapdragons.

In the centre of each table at the Wattle there were real flowers: gum-tips and luminous orange and yellow Iceland poppies in cut-glass vases, dropping their calyxes on the doilies as each new flower shook out its crumpled petals, the long hairy stems turning double-jointed in the water.

The speciality at the Wattle was Adelaide whiting, which all the ladies ordered if they didn't eat egg sandwiches or asparagus rolls. Afterwards there were scrumptious things on silver three-tiered cake stands: kisses, éclairs, butterfly cakes, neenish tarts, matches and lamingtons.

Sometimes, at the sound of too loud and imperious a voice at an adjacent table, or the appearance of a pink-cheeked man in a hound's-tooth jacket and corduroy trousers with perhaps, also, a spoilt child, behaving like a *little madam*, my mother, or one of the other seed-packets, would smile secretly at her neighbour and, with a roll of her eyes, mouth the mysterious initials, like a code: 'E.N.T.' The whisper ran around the Wattle; nudges and little moues were exchanged, serviettes would discreetly mask smiles as eyes swivelled in the direction of this rather stiff *loud* family. 'E.N.T. and no doubt about it I'm afraid, Coral!' I heard a tight-lipped Carnation exclaim to a Gladiolus. English Next Table.

Lou and Eric – my parents – belonged to the local tennis club and on Saturday afternoons I would sit in the small clubhouse with a book listening to the distant laughter from the mixed doubles and the soporific sounds of tennis floating in from the courts. After the tennis there was always an enormous tea dominated by something called a 'tennis cake'. They were carefree afternoons of perpetual sunshine which the war changed forever.

We lived quite close to the Camberwell Sports Ground and on Saturday afternoons, if I happened to be at home in bed sick, I would hear, borne with terrible clarity across the housetops, the spasmodic applause of the cricket fans and, worse, in winter, the frighteningly mindless roar of the football rabble. Long before I was ever forced by school authorities to

26

watch these horrible and pointless games, I had formed a life-long aversion to them based solely on those first auditory impressions. Crowds have always frightened and appalled me unless they happen to be in a theatre during one of my engagements. Then the noise they make is benign; a great ecstatic whoosh like a fire going up a chimney or the word 'yes' chanted by a heavenly host.

My mother was always concerned about my health and the great bogy of my childhood was Infantile Paralysis. I was never quite sure how old one had to be to avoid this scourge, nor had I ever met a victim, but I willingly swallowed whatever my mother poured into a spoon and pressed to my lips. Usually it was just the sticky and delicious Saunder's Malt Extract. I had seen it advertised on a hoarding which depicted a muscular baby, decorously diapered, shouldering an enormous steel girder. A favourite tonic of my mother's was Hypol, which was a less palatable white emulsion of cod-liver oil. There was, however, one prophylactic against Infantile Paralysis and other ailments that always made me sick. It was the egg flip, a glass of milk into which a raw egg had been whisked. Threads and clots of albumen always wrapped themselves around my uvula like a tourniquet, and although I gagged horribly, favours were withheld until I drank the last drop.

The illnesses of my childhood, although brief, gave me time to lie in bed, reading and listening to the wireless. My mother put the Radiola set in my room on a table beside the bed, and between sips of barley water I would tweak the knurled Bakelite knob from station to station. Throughout the day there was a succession of what are now called soap operas. Many of them employed the same actors, so that it was disquieting to hear a familiar character in *Aunt Jenny's Real Life Stories* crop up again with a different name in *Dr Mack*, *Fred and Maggie Everybody*, *When a Girl Marries* and *Martin's Corner*. Somehow it gave all those radio melodramas a spooky homogeneity.

In the mornings, soon after *Daybreak Dan*, there was a popular programme of community singing; a type of entertainment that has almost died out. With Uncle Wilf, Aunty Vi and John, I once went to a recording of this show in a small radio auditorium in town. It was thronged with women, a few accompanied by their children. Some of the ladies had brought knitting, very often khaki socks on five needles, and others had colanders in their laps into which they absently shelled peas. Led by a radio 'personality' called Charlie Vaud, with Mabel Nelson at the piano, they all enthusiastically sang such wartime hits as 'Run Rabbit Run', 'We're Going to Hang Out Our Washing on the Siegfried Line', 'Hey, Little Hen', 'Berlin or Bust' and 'The White Cliffs of Dover'. There was a vaudeville interlude when two comedians called Edgley and Dawe capered before the microphone and a strange woman called Nellie Colley, dressed in top hat and tails and smoking a pipe, sang a comic song called 'Burlington Bertie'. It was my first enticing glimpse of the Music Hall.

There were humorous interludes on the radio: mostly records of pre-war British vaudeville comics like George Tilly, Sid Field, Cyril Fletcher, Jack Hulbert and Cicely Courtneidge and my favourite, Horace Kenny. I would lie there in the darkened room through measles, mumps, whooping cough and scarlet fever, with my calamine lotion and Vicks Vaporub, laughing at those wonderful old-fashioned jesters. In the voices of some of these radio comics I recognized with a start the northern intonations of my father's father, whose Lancastrian accent had hitherto seemed so unique and outlandish. Here on the wireless were men with similar voices, interrupted by explosions of laughter. I later wondered why so many of the funniest comedians came from the North of England and why the idea of a 'Kent comic' seemed so anomalous.

In the forties, yodelling was popular and there were many excruciating hillbilly programmes on the wireless, but in the afternoon the children's sessions began, and I would listen to rather arch transmissions of *Chums at Chatterbox Corner* and later, around teatime, *The Search for the Golden Boomerang*, which used as its signature tune the voluptuous hothouse melody of Tchaikovsky's 'Waltz of the Flowers'. By the end of the day the bedroom smelt strongly of my medicaments mingled with the aroma of hot Bakelite.

One morning, when I was about ten, I woke very early, and as I went to the lavatory I glanced down at the skirting board outside my bedroom door. I then got down on my hands and knees and looked at it more closely. There was a small wire staple fixed to the wood an inch or two above the carpet, through which was threaded a thin cord. There was another staple on the opposite side of the architrave, and more, as I discovered, at regular intervals between my bedroom and the door to my parents' room, into which, like Ariadne's thread, the string disappeared. It occurred to me that I could easily have tripped on this filament on my way to the bathroom, and it was a mere fluke that I had not.

That morning, I was alone with my father for a few minutes after he had made my mother's breakfast, and when I told him of my strange discovery he became agitated and evasive. Finally, swearing me to secrecy, he explained that for some weeks he and my mother had been disturbed in the middle of the night by Barbara's sleepwalking, so he had installed this ingenious system of trip cords which connected to a bell beside his bed. Thus, whatever the hour, he would be instantly alerted to my sister's noctambulations and steer her safely back to bed. I must say, he looked particularly haggard that morning so I assumed the mechanism had been working all too successfully over the past few weeks.

I could not help but admire my father's ingenuity, though only one detail puzzled me; the cord did not pass across my sister's bedroom door, but mine. A few weeks later I noticed the whole system had been dismantled without a trace, and my father looked considerably rested in the mornings. I assumed that my unconscious wanderings had come to an end.

My father had secured a valuable contract to build a sausage factory for Mr Prince of Prince's Sausages. I went along with him to the old meat works for his first discussions. The noise in the factory was deafening and there was an appalling and nidorous smell. Very fat men in overalls and gumboots sloshed around in pink water as machines masticated huge quivering swags and chandeliers of offal; mauve, crimson and magenta. At the other end dirty pipes extruded serpents and stools of bright pink mince which the brutish men aimed into endless frankfurter skins. I remember my father had to rush away to be sick and thereafter never ate another sausage in his life. At our children's parties we always had cocktail frankfurters – from another firm – which we dunked in sauce and washed down with raspberry vinegar. These lavish teas, usually a celebration of a birthday, were held on Saturday afternoons and were preceded by a matinée at the Rivoli Picture Theatre near the Camberwell Junction. After the candles had been blown out and the last frankfurter ground into a slice of bread and butter and hundreds and thousands, there were party games in the garden until the parents arrived to escort their invariably weeping children home to be sick. Uncle Wilf always turned up at my parties and would organize the activities, which sometimes got rather rough, and he would find himself playing 'Stacks on the Mill, More on Still' flat on his back on the lawn beneath a writhing pyramid of about fifteen small boys.

> 'Stacks on the mill,
> More on still . . .'

chanted the children. My parents would exchange a glance and my mother once said, 'Poor Wilf. He loves children and he's only got John.'

Uncle Wilf always bought the latest parlour games which helped to fill in the long evenings after tea when we were up at Healesville. We loved Mah-jong until Wilf produced a pack of Belisha, a new card game inspired by British traffic signs. Each card had a picturesque view of England, Scotland or Wales painted in bright colours in a slightly primitive, 31

Lowry-ish style. Although the cars in the pictures looked quaintly out of date, the landscapes, as green as salads, and the castles and thatched cottages, filled me with a yearning to go there.

After the family weekend at the shack, we used to drive back from Healesville in rather a long convoy, stopping occasionally for the children to go behind bushes or for Aunt Ella to be sick, or sometimes stopping too for Uncle Wilf to get out of their grey Chev and lean for a while with his elbows on the roof and his head in his hands. We would stop our car a few yards ahead and my father would watch his brother-in-law in the rear-vision mirror. 'Wilf's getting more of those headaches,' he said. 'Time he had a check-up.' A few months later he did, and had to go to hospital for a 'minor operation', as my parents, with their usual prudery about illness, described the removal of a brain tumour. I spoke to him on the telephone soon after he came home from the Alfred Hospital but he didn't seem to know who I was. When he died, leaving no will, the house and the land at Healesville had to be sold to provide money for his widow and son. And we left the bush forever.

Not long after Wilf's funeral, which I was not allowed to attend, my father and I were driving to one of his more important jobs to deliver a precious cargo of plate glass which was roped to the open boot. My father was driving a little too fast and as we went over an unexpected hump in the road there was an ominous thump and a dull crash behind the car. My father pulled over to the side of the road and got out to examine the disaster. I had never heard him swear, but this time he stood looking at the shivered panes and released a litany of curses. Then he sat on the kerb and sobbed quietly for a while. I didn't know what to do, but I felt he wasn't just grieving over the glass.

Hats and Glads

Camberwell Grammar School had been built in the grounds of a large Victorian house in an older neighbouring suburb. The original gardens were still there, including two elephantine Moreton Bay fig trees and a tottering arbour, from which, in its season, wistaria mauvely dripped. There was also the inevitable Norfolk Island pine tree which every Victorian residence of any distinction seemed to possess. They rose like tall viridian fishbones over the suburban landscape and always denoted the presence of an interesting old house. Today, however, though many of the trees survive, their gardens are often subdivided and the houses demolished; replaced by nice 'units' and practical townhouses. Mr Tonkin, the magenta-nosed headmaster, lived in the original Victorian house in the school grounds that also accommodated a few wretched and dispossessed boarders on whom we well-fed, warmly housed day boys gazed with pity.

My teachers in the junior school were mostly women. But there was a bald and nervous little choirmaster called Mr Dennis who visited the school and led us all in rousing renditions of 'Nymphs and Shepherds', 'Bird of the Wilderness' (... blithesome and cumberless) and a muscular ditty called 'Clang, Clang, Clang on the Anvil' – a song that sounded particularly odd when rendered by boy sopranos. At home Purcell's 'Nymphs and Shepherds' became my earliest party turn, after my mother had overheard me singing it in the bath, and much to my embarrassment she insisted that I sing it to all the uncles and aunts at the next family Sunday tea party. I only agreed to this on condition I was allowed to perform behind the curtain, so that my voice was disembodied like those on the radio. Thereafter, if ever my parents wanted to cajole me into a song or recitation, they would have to say – and I wince to recall the words – *pretend to be the wireless*. Needless to say I have pretended to be the wireless on many occasions since.

After the persecutions by Miss Jensen at my former school, Camberwell Grammar was a blissful respite, though a boy called John Bromley, who seemed tall for his age and had soft white skin like a slug, used to push me over whenever he saw me, for no reason that I could ever understand. I learnt to avoid him . . .

Sometimes when Bromley's capricious bullying got too much for me I would, I am afraid, seek a victim of my own. There was a perfectly nice, but rather small lad called Gifford, whom I pushed over a couple of times, on one occasion causing his mother's beautifully cut sandwiches to scatter on the dusty playground. For years afterwards I experienced a sharp pang of guilt whenever I thought of this incident until, on a recent visit to Melbourne, I could bear it no longer and decided, half a century later, to make amends. By consulting the telephone directory I discovered that there was, in fact, a Bruce Gifford who was practising architecture in the city and to my delight he answered the telephone. I came quickly to the point, explaining that I was sorry about the sandwiches and hoped he was doing well and that there were no hard feelings. A wave of relief and absolution passed over me, though as I gently replaced the receiver, I could still hear his voice exclaiming, 'Who is this? Who *is* this?'

I loved history, art and English, but I was already having difficulty with arithmetic, which seemed to be the one subject in which my father hoped I might excel. Even then I may have been vaguely aware that he wanted me to become an architect; something better and grander than himself. If only he had known, he could have adopted little Gifford!

One morning, through the classroom window, we noticed a strange figure prowling around outside in the school playground. He wore floppy green trousers, a red shirt and a bow tie, and his hair was very long and wavy. We laughed delightedly at the sight of him; he was the oddest fellow any of us had ever seen. Miss Ewers left the classroom and went outside and we saw her talking to the peculiar stranger for a few minutes and shaking her head. They could both see our grinning faces pressed to the window and the weird man glanced at us nervously, but Miss Ewers did not seem to mind. She was blushing, and trying not to smile herself. Soon the stranger walked off towards the school gate and our teacher came back into the classroom. She sat at her desk and exploded with laughter. She was convulsed. 'Who was that, Miss?' we all asked, but Miss Ewers took some time to compose herself. 'He . . . wanted to know if we'd like him to give us theatre lessons at the school!' She could hardly get the words out before a further paroxysm. We were all laughing now and the

weird man must have heard us through one of the open

windows. We could see him at the gate, gazing back at the school with a pale puzzled face. 'Who is he, Miss Ewers?' we piped in chorus. Miss Ewers had gone bright red. She looked very pretty with her eyes sparkling with tears. 'An actor,' she said at last, drying her eyes with a handkerchief, 'he said he was an actor!' Our peals of merriment must surely have reached him now as he closed the gate and trudged off towards the bus stop.

Sport was my greatest problem at school. I was always perfectly healthy and yet I could never see the point of games. Paradoxically, I attribute my excellent constitution and energy today to the fact that since school I have never engaged in more than a minute of athletic activity. We all had to traipse down to a horrible building called The Gym. Here were coarse unscalable ropes, parallel bars and porridge-coloured mattresses, stained and pinguid from generations of brilliantined scalps and sweaty somersaults. This torture chamber was presided over by a man called Scotty, one of those repulsive and nuggety Caledonians with pale sandy hair and white eyelashes that gave him the look of a near-albino. Scotty was perpetually dressed in a short-sleeved Aertex, briefs and tennis shoes, which we called 'sandshoes' and 'ordinary' people called 'runners'. Scotty's piggy little eye fell on me immediately when he saw the difficulty I had in executing a pointless somersault. Much given to jocular nicknames, he decided that mine should be 'Granny Humphries', a soubriquet which met with the ribald approval of my schoolfellows. Needless to say, on subsequent sports days at which I was a reluctant participant and in the tedious brutalities of egg, spoon and sack races, the air   37 rang with shrill cries of 'Come on Granny! Come on Granny!' As the reader may imagine, I had little affection for Mr Scott, but I am happy to say that very many years later a terrible sadness befell him in which I played a decisive, if anonymous, role.

An unpleasant concomitant of Physical Training was the cold shower we were forced to endure in a dank concrete basement near the gym. There were no lights and no proper drainage system, so we had to splash around in the dark with black water up to our knees, for no good reason that I could comprehend, except that cold showers were supposed to be 'good for you'.

There was a tuck shop at the school where two women sold pasties and pies to boys whose mothers, unlike mine, could not be bothered to cut their sandwiches or lovingly pack their leather satchels with fruit and cakes. The savoury effluvium which wafted from the tuck shop daily at twelve o'clock percolated to every corner of the school, and as I chewed my bland sandwiches I sometimes wished I was just slightly neglected, as I hankered for a succulent pasty, haemorrhaging sauce.

It would not be long before we would all be officially urged to devour something called the 'Oslo lunch'. At the time I assumed this to be identical with the lunches eaten by schoolchildren in occupied Norway. It consisted of a carrot, a slice of brown bread (in Melbourne, in those days, this was white bread coloured brown), a piece of Kraft processed cheese still half-wrapped in foil and bearing a parent's thumb print, and half a pint of milk. For a short while in the early years of the war my mother followed this edict and daily packed this austere and unappetizing collation in my satchel. However, on the journey to school the milk bottle often leaked and by the end of the term most of our school bags reeked with the smell of raw leather, ink and rancid milk. Soon, and in spite of the war effort, I persuaded my mother to supply me with a normal lunch of spaghetti sandwiches and cakes.

At the beginning of the war with Japan, trenches were dug in the gardens of the old school house and we were issued with gas masks and strange black rubber gags which, if bitten on when the bombs fell, would prevent our teeth from shattering. We all had to bring money to school to pay for these prophylactics, but I horrified the Head and was made to feel shamefully unpatriotic when, before the whole school, I innocently asked whether we would get our money back if the Japs didn't bomb us. It was a solecism I was never allowed to forget.

Meanwhile the school grounds became a muddy maze of trenches, and strips of cellophane were pasted in lattice patterns all over the windows. On the wireless Vera Lynn optimistically sang:

> When the lights go on again
> All over the world . . .

Many of our neighbours in Christowell Street were happily building air-raid shelters in their back gardens. These were exciting subterranean dwellings upholstered with sandbags, but my father refused to disfigure our back lawn and constructed an elaborate, but barely bomb-proof, bunker under the stairs. Carpenters made large hardboard panels that could be fitted to the inside of our windows in the event of aerial bombardment, though how this could be done at high speed in an air raid, and in a house that must have had at least forty windows, is difficult to imagine. Fortunately it was never put to the test. The back garden was converted from flowers to vegetables and fruits, and in a short time we were producing our own carrots, parsnips, beans, potatoes, peas, lemons, peaches and apricots.

There was some confusion, certainly amongst children, as to which war we should be worrying about: the Hitler one or the Tojo one. However, most streets had a Fat for Britain depot.

It was popularly believed that fat, or its absence, would be a decisive factor in the outcome of the European war, and that the more fat we could send to England the better her chances of victory. The dripping from every Sunday roast in Melbourne was therefore carefully decanted into suitable containers – old Farex tins, glucose canisters and jam jars – and these, hygienically sealed, were left on the front porch of Mrs Long's Spanish Mission Home on the corner of Fairmont Avenue, whence they were presumably collected, consolidated and shipped to London. To this day I have never met a recipient or beneficiary of this lardy largesse, but the Japanese sank many Fat for Britain ships and it is strange to think of this greasy residue of a million Sunday joints lying in some coral dell at the bottom of the Pacific, waiting to produce the biggest dripping slick in history.

Our vicar, Canon P. W. Robinson, was a Londoner, and his sermons rambled on at some length about the threat to what was then called The Old Country and the safety of the King,

Queen and the little Princesses. To my father's disappointment, my mother always thought of some excuse for not going to church, though I knew that our sanctimonious vicar was the principal reason for her absence from Morning Prayer. My father, however, was a regular churchgoer, later a vestryman, and during the Offertory he would always slip a crunched-up pound note into the plate amongst everyone else's shillings, and insisted on saying Grace before meals: 'Forwhatweare-abouttoreceivemaytheLordmakeustrulythankfulAmen.' This always embarrassed me when we had friends to stay, as my father's recitation usually caught them unawares mid-way through the first forkful. And sometimes, at night, I would see him through their half-open bedroom door – it was rarely closed – kneeling in prayer beside the bed. Canon Robinson took a great fancy to me and always patted my head vigorously after Sunday service. I had the uncomfortable feeling, later confirmed, that he envisaged some future for me in the Ministry, and at Sunday school he was always singling me out to read the lesson.

Sunday was the worst day of the week, because my father, with his north of England Methodist upbringing, forbade us to play with any other children on the Sabbath. Instead there were endless drives back and forth to St Mark's rather ugly buff-stuccoed nave, and the cold red-brick Sunday school beside it. In church, I liked the music, though I successfully resisted Canon Robinson's efforts to conscript me into the choir. However, the smell of everybody's 'Sunday Best'; the camphor, the talcum, hair oil and the toilet water, mingled with whatever disinfectant it was that the cleaners used, always made me feel like passing out as if I had inhaled carbon monoxide. Withal I struggled for some great faith; some transcendental religious experience. Great-Uncle Albert, always extolled to me as the most successful member of the Humphries family, had, back in Manchester, once written a seminal work, *The Holy Spirit in Faith and Experience* (Primitive Methodist Publishing Company, 1911), and though I attempted to read this book many times, it failed to yield up its mystery to me. Moreover, there was some evidence from its musty unopened appearance that previous readers had also abandoned their search for Truth amongst the closely printed pages.

Sunday lunch – or dinner as it was called – always consisted of a Roast; lamb, pork or beef. This was always cooked, as I still prefer it, until it was an attractive shade of grey. The roast was accompanied by potatoes, parsnips and pumpkin baked to a crisp, the pumpkin caramelized. This would be followed by tinned peaches or a steamed pudding in which apricot jam, golden syrup or sultanas were alternating constituents. Much as I looked forward to this meal throughout the tedious tracts of Canon Robinson's sermon, I dreaded the return home as well. For Sunday was the day that my parents usually had 'words'. It would be more truthful to say that they had no words at all, but there was a palpable atmosphere of tension which had no explicable origin. It may have been that my parents, to all appearances a happily married couple, found the prospect of one day in the week spent in each other's company unendurable. This oppressive atmosphere, which froze the heart of a child, may have had a purely gastric origin, as we consumed those large quantities of fat that would never find their way to Britain. Happily, the family's spirits lifted at last when we piled into the Oldsmobile and later the Buick and went for the traditional Sunday-afternoon spin.

There was nothing my parents enjoyed more than motoring around the new suburbs on the outskirts of the town looking at houses. For my father, the builder, it was an excursion of professional interest, and every now and then, as we drove down a brand-new street of villas, with their freshly planted lawns, bird baths and sickly silver birches, he might suddenly jam on the brakes and point an enraged finger at some crude, jerry-built imitation of one of his own designs. On the new roads, crescents and boulevards flanked by pristine triple-fronted cream-brick bungalows, other vehicles filled with gawking families also cruised. It was the thing everyone did on a Sunday afternoon, and it was called *Looking at the Lovely Homes*. On the hills of Ivanhoe and Eaglemont above the Yarra River, where the artists of the 1880s had painted their idyllic 'impressions', stood some of the grander new houses with tennis courts which especially interested my mother. Mostly of brick, the colour of milky tea, they had curved nautical-looking terraces, balconies and picture windows, with satin festoon or 'veil of tears' blinds; and if these were raised, as they often were by the proud owners, there might be a glimpse within of blond veneer and peach mirror, and prowling along the window sill just inside the glass, a lithe white marble puma.

The lovely homes bored me. As we glided along in our big chubby car past the raw new houses, still smelling of wet cement, admiring the azaleas and the 'crazy' stone work, the 'feature' chimneys and the names of the houses or their street 43 numbers scribbled across the façades in duck-egg blue wrought-iron, I hankered for hovels. There was a place I had heard of called Dudley Flats, a low-lying wasteland to the west of Melbourne, where 'slums' and *really* poor people could be found.

I begged my parents to drive me there so that I could see them for myself. But we never visited the older suburbs of Melbourne, except when we went to see my mother's sister, Ella, who still lived in a dark Victorian house in Thornbury where her parents had once lived and my mother had grown up. It had ruby and Bristol-blue glass in the panels beside the front door and a long central corridor with a curtain half-way down, so that when the front door was opened, visitors were not afforded a vulgar view of the back yard. There was even an aspidistra in the front parlour which Ella washed with milk, and I once asked my father, in the presence of my aunt and uncle, if their house was a *real* hovel.

Sometimes on Sunday afternoons we would visit the Melbourne General Cemetery with my relations on my mother's side. After much wandering through the maze of granite obelisks and tottering tombstones, overrun with skeleton weed and lantana, we came to a grave that was better kept than the rest. It looked rather like a narrow bed of grey stone, covered with marble chips, and on the headstone was my grandmother's name. My mother removed the old stalks and put some fresh flowers in a little vase buried in the gravel. Aunty Elsie pulled out the weeds and we all just stood and shuffled, looking at the grave and trying to feel something. Around us were sadly neglected plots and even a few that had caved in, so that kneeling down and peering through the cracks you might just see the skeletons of other people's grandmothers.

To earn extra pocket money I often went shopping for my mother. There was a small parade of shops not far away in Camberwell Road, and although their proprietors, Mr Hall, the grocer, Mr Ryal, the chemist, and Mr Ernie Young, the butcher, all seemed to me to be of normal height, my mother always referred to them as diminutive. 'Barry, would you please go down the street and get me a half a pound of nice lean lamb chops from my little butcher. Oh, and while you're there, pop in and ask the little man in the chemist shop for a bottle of Hypol and some Buckley's Canadiol Mixture.' I always took a basket with an orange ten-shilling note and a ration book.

There seemed to be no great shortage of anything, though butterless recipes were popular, but I would stand on the sawdust floor of little Mr Young's butcher's shop while he put his bloodied thumbs in a pair of scissors and deftly snipped a few squares off our meat-ration book. Sometimes, if there was a big card night looming, I could pick up a sponge, a lemon meringue pie or a few fairy cakes from the Misses Longmire who had the 'homemade' cake shop at the end of the Parade. There was always a delicious smell in their shop, though it puzzled me, since everything was baked on the premises, that the Misses Longmire could, with a clear conscience, describe their confections as being homemade when they were so obviously baked in a shop.

If I were not running simple errands after school, I might be in my laboratory mixing quite dangerous combinations of 45 sulphur and potassium permanganate over a spirit burner or practising a few magic tricks. I had always had a hankering to be a magician like the top-hatted, opera-cloaked gigolo called Mandrake who appeared regularly in a comic strip in my mother's *Women's Weekly*. Mandrake had only to 'gesture hypnotically' and people disappeared. That seemed to me to be the greatest gift imaginable; to make people and things vanish.

Sometimes, too, I might even play with my sister and her little friends, Maurine and Valerie. My mother had long ago whispered to me that Valerie was adopted, but never to say anything to her face because her adoptive parents had not yet told her. At the time this information intrigued and frightened me, since it occurred to me that I, like Val, might also be adopted and that my parents too could be keeping this a secret. It even occurred to me that my mother's confidences about Val's origins might be her way of preparing the ground for a confession of her own. It was true to say that her expressions of love for me were sometimes evasive or ambiguous. Once when I was quite young I asked her point-blank if she loved me and she seemed nonplussed and embarrassed. 'Well,' she replied evasively, 'naturally I love your father most of all, and then *my* mother and father, and after that, you and your sister, just the same.' It was clear from what she said that love had a strictly hierarchical structure, and was certainly not something that could be spontaneously experienced or bestowed. My unspoken adoption fears were not put to rest when my mother said, as she frequently did to others in my presence: 'Eric and I don't know *where Barry comes from*.' I have recorded this story as accurately as I can recollect it in order to show the warmer side of my mother's complex personality.

Every now and then there were special occasions; usually a wedding, or a dance at the tennis club. Weeks before these events my mother and I would drive to a distant suburb to the home of Miss Wilmot, my mother's dressmaker, and I would wait in the hall while she had another 'fitting'. These seemed to take forever, and from time to time, Miss Wilmot would put her head around the door and smile at me reassuringly, as if that were possible with a mouthful of pins. Taffeta was my mother's favourite fabric in that epoch; it was before the age of Thai silk. Taffeta was cool and it rustled and chafed upon itself, and before my mother's big night out it was, with a few drops of Bond Street perfume, the nicest textile to say your prayers against.

Once they went to a grand luncheon at the Town Hall, and my mother wore her best suit from Mitzi of Vienna, and a hat with a veil covered with fat black polka dots. Later I asked her what it was like. 'Lovely,' she replied. 'I'm pleased I went to a bit of trouble. It was all hats and glads.'

Gladioli, especially flesh-pink ones, were the floral symbols of respectability, success and thrusting, unquestioning optimism. They also seemed somehow to be the appropriate emblems of Mr Menzies, the reigning prime minister, who had such a nice 'speaking voice'. Never before had I heard a voice so described, and when my parents tuned in to the wireless to hear one of his public addresses I listened attentively to those sanctimonious, lah-di-dah tones, trying to detect why my

47

parents had singled out this 'speaking voice' in particular. Did he have other more recondite voices, I wondered wickedly. A farting voice perhaps? Above all, Mr Menzies was extolled by my parents and their friends for his repartee and the swiftness with which he rebuked interjections from the Opposition supporters, whom he wittily described as 'that riff-raff at the back of the hall' to roars of laughter and applause.

His opponent, who was later victorious, was Mr Chifley, 'a pipe-smoking Labourite', who had once, Mrs Kendall whispered, 'been a *train driver*'. Certainly Mr Chifley had nothing which could be described as a 'speaking voice', and my father summed him up in three words, 'rough as bags'. 'Irish, too,' my mother added tartly. Since her only brother had married a Roman Catholic and been ostracized, my mother had little affection for the Irish. 'But didn't Nana's mother come from Ireland?' I asked ingenuously. '*Northern* Ireland, Barry,' she averred warmly, 'that's the nice part of Ireland, and don't you forget it.'

I sometimes think I might still bear the ugly scars of my early indoctrination, when I read absurdly Anglophobic accounts of the Gallipoli Campaign and sensationalist works of Australian history like Robert Hughes's *The Fatal Shore*, where the British are uniformly depicted as shits, and the Irish convicts as misunderstood scallywags and political prisoners. 'He would write that, wouldn't he,' I reflect, 'typical revisionist Mick that he is!' A modern manifestation of this persistent sectarian split in Australian life is the Republican Movement with its cant about patriotism. It is, of course, no such thing, but just another form of pommy-bashing. One has only to glance at the names of its most vociferous champions: Keating, Keneally, Doherty, O'Horne. It is no surprise that the Australian Republican flag is green.

Today I keep my sweaters in a toffee-coloured chest lined with camphor wood. It is densely and rather crudely carved with dragons and ovate oriental bas-reliefs which I remember in the greatest detail from my earliest childhood. It was bought by my grandparents in Colombo as they returned from the Coronation on the Orient Line, as, indeed, were thousands more identical chests purchased by other voyagers. It used to stand in our upstairs hallway and contained my mother's best things: her furs, rugs, table linen, wedding dress, and a gold meshed evening belt encrusted with imitation rubies, sapphires and emeralds.

When I was eleven I noticed in the window of a small second-hand shop near Camberwell Junction a pair of earrings that seemed to match my mother's belt perfectly. I covertly inquired the price which, though I no longer recall it, may have been quite expensive for such cheap paste, but over a long period, and by secretly slipping into the shop and leaving small amounts, I finally paid off the earrings, brought them home and carefully hid them. As her birthday approached I wrapped the earrings, speculating excitedly on the surprise and delight they would bring. I had not even breathed a word to my sister or father.

The great morning came and my father brought my mother breakfast in bed. It was then that I proudly presented my small package. I watched my mother's face carefully as she 49 unwrapped it, but when the tissue paper parted and she saw the earrings, she did not smile. Instead her face darkened and she turned angrily to my father. 'Where did he get these, Eric?' my mother said sharply. 'I hope he didn't pay for these out of his own money?' My father looked confused, and speechless. 'Where did you get them?' my mother asked me. 'Not from that little rogue down at the Junction, I hope. How much did they cost?' I muttered a price. 'Daylight robbery,' exploded my mother. She thrust the earrings at my father. 'Eric?' she commanded. 'I want you to go straight down to that little Jew and tell him to give Barry his money back. And you can also tell him if he goes on overcharging children for rubbish like this I'll have him reported.' Needless to say, that was one of my mother's more memorable birthdays.

My father often used to bring home carnations as a peace offering for some nameless transgression, and I always found them unsympathetic flowers: prim, sharply budded, pinked and serrated blooms in ice-cream colours, with a scent that smelled sprayed-on. They still fill me with a remote dread. Always wrapped in a cone of pink or purple tissue paper, they often lay on the hall table for a long while, depending on the time my mother had set for my father's sentence. But in the end she would always drop them in a vase and say with a smile, 'Look at the lovely carnations your father has given me.' They had worked again.

My father insisted that my mother have domestic help. I had never quite recovered from the sudden departure of my first beloved nanny, Edna, who left without farewells or adequate

50

explanations; although later there was a succession of domestics and housekeepers, they never meant the same to me. After my brother Michael was born my mother engaged a girl from the nearby Salvation Army home, euphoniously called Valmai Grubb. Although my mother admitted that the rest of Valmai's family were almost certainly 'ordinary', Valmai, she insisted, had a very kind heart and a sweet soft nature. Why otherwise would she cry so uncontrollably when rebuked? Valmai stayed a long time and was replaced by Mrs Lane, a woman of about sixty, who came from Welshpool and whom my mother described as 'very countrified'. They took an instant dislike to each other and my mother told me that as soon as she saw the down-trodden heels of Mrs Lane's shoes she knew that she should never have engaged her. On Mrs Lane's days off my mother would inspect the floor of the shower recess and with some satisfaction she always found it to be dry and the room filled with a cloying scent of Three Flowers talcum powder, Mrs Lane's preferred alternative to soap and water. In the mornings, as the housekeeper trudged up the stairs with my mother's breakfast tray, my sister and I often overheard her muttering under her frequently juniper-scented breath the malediction: 'I hate her, I hate her, *I hate her*.'

Having engaged a 'home help' who had quickly proved herself unsuitable, my mother found herself unable to dismiss her, so that thereafter Mrs Lane, having failed as a housekeeper, was retained – even became indispensable – as an example of incompetence and slovenliness. 'Look at the dust,' my mother would say with some satisfaction. 'It's that grub Mrs Lane. She thinks I don't notice.' My mother confided all her complaints about Mrs Lane to Mrs Shores, the woman who came to do the washing and ironing. Mrs Shores was a garrulous lady with a shrill laugh and a husband who enjoyed a drink. She laughed immoderately, though quite genuinely, at all my mother's sardonic jokes. Whenever Mrs Shores arrived my mother would hurry to impart to her Mrs Lane's latest outrage, at which Mrs Shores would burst into peals of incredulous hilarity. It began to look as though Mrs Lane would never be sacked, but be retained forever as a grim cabaret turn and an essential topic of conversation. Mrs Shores was another comic act on the same bill who frequently interrupted her tasks in the laundry to follow my amused parent from room to room gossiping; or she would stand in the kitchen recounting some long anecdote at the top of her voice, assuming my mother was listening in the adjacent sun-room. However my mother often went upstairs, or wandered into the garden to pick a few camellias, and after a wink at me would return to the house to find Mrs Shores still cheerfully soliloquizing.

Mr Dunt, the gardener, was another incompetent hired in order to provide my mother with anecdotes of incompetence. He was an old man, though perhaps little older than the author of this memoir, who arrived on a bicycle with a large pannier attached to the handlebars and who thereafter pottered about pruning the wrong things and digging up carefully planted bulbs. Mr Dunt had a special cup and saucer for his afternoon tea, from which we were forbidden to drink since it was rather uncertain as to where Mr Dunt might have been. It was only after a few years that my father noticed that small things were missing from his workshop behind the garage. The absence of an expensive electric exhaust fan finally aroused his suspicions and a telephone call was made to Mr Dunt's family who, sure enough, discovered a large haul of unused appliances, as well as hinges, nails, trowels and hammers, under the old man's bed. We never saw him again.

One day when I was about six my mother disappeared. My young sister and I were given no explanation of this terrible event and a kind family friend called Janet Ballantyne came to look after us. My father was rarely home, and seemed so stricken with anxiety that we were unable to demand an explanation. I would lie in bed feeling as though some calamity had taken place. Somehow it was even uncertain whether my mother would ever return. But she did. Perhaps she had only been absent for a few weeks, and quite recently I learnt that she had suffered a miscarriage and spent a period convalescing in hospital. My family were madly circumspect in matters to do with illness, sex and even reality, so that a misfortune combining all three taboos was veiled in absolute silence. To this day I can remember those feelings of childish desolation, so that if people close to me leave me now, even on shopping expeditions, I always need to know exactly where they are going, or that oppressive intimation of loss, with all its old force, comes back to me.

ISABEL ALLENDE · *Voices in My Ear*

NICHOLSON BAKER · *Playing Trombone*

LINDSEY BAREHAM · *The Little Book of Big Soups*

KAREN BLIXEN · *From the Ngong Hills*

DIRK BOGARDE · *Coming of Age*

ANTHONY BURGESS · *Childhood*

ANGELA CARTER · *Lizzie Borden*

CARLOS CASTANEDA · *The Sorcerer's Ring of Power*

ELIZABETH DAVID · *Peperonata and Other Italian Dishes*

RICHARD DAWKINS · *The Pocket Watchmaker*

GERALD DURRELL · *The Pageant of Fireflies*

RICHARD ELLMANN · *The Trial of Oscar Wilde*

EPICURUS · *Letter on Happiness*

MARIANNE FAITHFULL · *Year One*

KEITH FLOYD · *Hot and Spicy Floyd*

ALEXANDER FRATER · *Where the Dawn Comes Up Like Thunder*

ESTHER FREUD · *Meeting Bilal*

JOHN KENNETH GALBRAITH · *The Culture of Contentment*

ROB GRANT AND DOUG NAYLOR · *Scenes from the Dwarf*

ROBERT GRAVES · *The Gods of Olympus*

JANE GRIGSON · *Puddings*

SOPHIE GRIGSON · *From Sophie's Table*

KATHARINE HEPBURN · *Little Me*

SUSAN HILL · *The Badness Within Him*

ALAN HOLLINGHURST · *Adventures Underground*

BARRY HUMPHRIES · *Less is More Please*

HOWARD JACOBSON · *Expulsion from Paradise*

P. D. JAMES · *The Girl Who Loved Graveyards*

STEPHEN KING · *Umney's Last Case*

LAO TZU · *Tao Te Ching*

DAVID LEAVITT · *Chips Is Here*

PENGUIN 60s